TECHNOLOGY MYTHS,
BUSTED!

by Angie Smibert

12 STORY LIBRARY

www.12StoryLibrary.com

12-Story Library is an imprint of Peterson Publishing Company and Press Room Editions.

Produced for 12-Story Library by Red Line Editorial

Photographs ©: SpeedKingz/Shutterstock Images, cover, 1, 29; LeFebvre Communications/PA Wire URN:13330675/AP Images, 4; 3DDock/Shutterstock Images, 7; Alfonso de Tomas/Shutterstock Images, 8; Eric Risberg/AP Images, 9; Daimond Shutter/Shutterstock Images, 10; US Navy, 11; Nanisimova/Shutterstock Images, 12; Bloomua/Shutterstock Images, 13; Phil Reid/Shutterstock Images, 14; Roman Pyshchyk/Shutterstock Images, 15; Pelfophoto/Shutterstock Images, 16; jumpinzon/Shutterstock Images, 17, 28; Monkey Business Images/Shutterstock Images, 18; Oleksandr Berezko/Shutterstock Images, 19; Stockbyte/Thinkstock, 20; Photographee.eu/Shutterstock Images, 21; Lucky Business/Shutterstock Images, 22; Sylvie Bouchard/Shutterstock Images, 23; Art Konovalov/Shutterstock Images, 24; J. Lekavicius/Shutterstock Images, 25; nito/Shutterstock Images, 26; Twin Design/Shutterstock Images, 27

Library of Congress Cataloging-in-Publication Data
Names: Smibert, Angie, author.
Title: Technology myths, busted! / by Angie Smibert.
Description: North Mankato, MN : 12-Story Library, [2017] | Series: Science
  myths, busted! | Audience: Grades 4 to 6. | Includes bibliographical
  references and index.
Identifiers: LCCN 2016002368| ISBN 9781632353061 (library bound : alk. paper)
  | ISBN 9781632353566 (pbk. : alk. paper)
Subjects: LCSH: Technology--Miscellanea--Juvenile literature. | Errors,
  Scientific--Juvenile literature.
Classification: LCC T48 .S65 2017 | DDC 602--dc23
LC record available at http://lccn.loc.gov/2016002368

Printed in the United States of America
Mankato, MN
May, 2016

Table of Contents

1

Busted: The World Wide Web and the Internet Are Identical

Many people use the terms *World Wide Web* and *Internet* to mean the same thing. But these systems are not the same. The World Wide Web is a part of the Internet.

The Internet is a global network of computers. They are linked together by several protocols. Protocols are special sets of rules. They tell computers and other devices how to talk to each other.

The Internet is actually a network of networks. It began its life as a

THINK ABOUT IT

Based on what you read, what is the difference between the Internet and the Web?

Tim Berners-Lee invented the World Wide Web in 1989.

military-sponsored research network. The military created the Advanced Research Project Agency Network (ARPANET) in 1969. In the 1970s and 1980s, ARPANET expanded. It included universities and other research organizations throughout the world. In the late 1980s, the Internet became public. Everyone could use it. It included a variety of ways to communicate or move files around. Users could e-mail, transfer files, participate in newsgroups, and chat together.

In 1989, Tim Berners-Lee designed a new way to share information on the Internet. He called it the

World Wide Web. It was simple, yet revolutionary. He built a Web page that displayed text and photographs. But most important, it linked to other pages. This created a web of information. The World Wide Web is made up of servers. Servers are computers that store Web pages, photographs, and videos. These servers are part of the much larger Internet. Without the Internet, the Web could not exist.

In 1990, the first Web browser was created. It kicked off decades of growth for the Web. Today, the Web is huge. People use Web browsers such as Google Chrome and Internet Explorer to navigate it. But it makes up only a portion of the vast Internet. The Internet also includes peer-to-peer file sharing and instant messaging. It includes video and audio streaming and gaming. It also includes e-mail and chat. Video streaming is using more and more of the Internet's bandwidth. Netflix is a video streaming service. It accounts for 35 percent of Internet traffic.

966 million

Estimated number of live websites as of December 2015.

- The Internet began as a military research network in 1969.
- Berners-Lee invented the World Wide Web in 1989.
- The World Wide Web is a part of the Internet.

2

Busted: The QWERTY Keyboard Just Kept Keys from Jamming

In 1867, newspaper editor Christopher Sholes patented the typewriter. Until recently, most historians thought he designed the keyboard to prevent jams. Sholes first tried arranging the letters alphabetically. But typists found the metal keys got stuck together when they typed quickly. So Sholes rearranged the keyboard. The sequence he created is called *QWERTY*. Today's keyboards use this layout.

Sholes did redesign the keyboard to make it easier for users. But the problem was not stuck keys. It was typing efficiency. Recently, researchers discovered Sholes actually may have redesigned the keyboard for telegraph operators.

They were the first people to use Sholes's typewriters. They typed out messages in Morse code. This code uses specific letter combinations. Some combinations are used more than others. The operators used S, Z, and E frequently. So Sholes moved those letters closer together.

DVORAK KEYBOARDS

In the 1930s, August Dvorak designed a keyboard. Its middle row of keys includes the most common letters in English. These letters are A O E U I D H T N S. The majority of English words use one or more of these letters. Dvorak claimed this made typing easier and faster. Today, the Dvorak keyboard is rarely used.

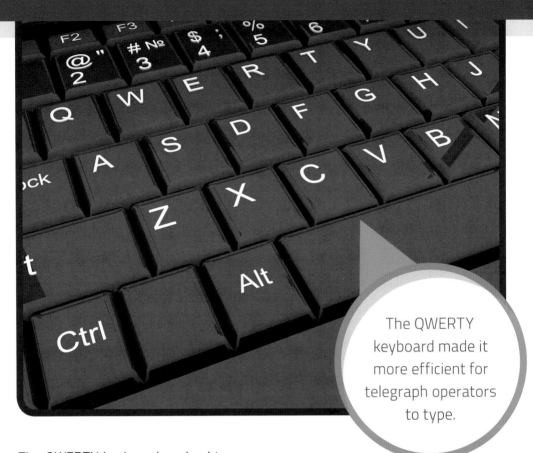

The QWERTY keyboard made it more efficient for telegraph operators to type.

The QWERTY keyboard evolved to help the telegraph operators type faster. Later, teletype machines adopted the keyboard the operators were already familiar with: QWERTY. Sholes also made a deal with Remington to sell his typewriters. They became widely used. The QWERTY keyboard has stuck around until this day. But it was not invented in response to stuck keys.

100,000
Number of typewriters with QWERTY keyboards used in the United States by 1890.

- Christopher Sholes patented the typewriter in 1867.
- The QWERTY keyboard evolved to help telegraph operators type faster.
- Most keyboards today still follow the same layout.

Busted:
Apple Computers
Cannot Get Viruses

For years, Apple users believed their computers were immune to viruses and malware. However, this was never true. A virus can attack any type of computer. A virus is a piece of computer code. It infects a computer and makes copies of itself. It makes changes within the computer, often doing harm. Users download viruses when they click on attachments from unknown sources.

In fact, the first personal computer attacked by a virus was an Apple II. In 1982, a 15-year-old hacker wrote the Elk Cloner Virus. It infected the Apple II and inserted a short poem into its code. In 1987, the first virus written for a Windows PC spread to an Apple. This prompted the first antivirus software for a Macintosh.

So how did the Apple myth start? In the 2000s, Apple released an ad campaign. In one of its ads, it claimed Apple computers did not get viruses. But this was not true. Apple computers did get fewer viruses than some other computers did. But not

Many Apple users believed their computers were immune from attack.

A 15-year-old hacker wrote a virus for the Apple II in 1982.

because the Apple computers were immune. Apple computers were less popular than Windows PCs. Hackers wanted to infect the most computers they could. They wrote viruses to attack Windows PCs, ignoring Apple ones. Then, Apple computers became more popular. Viruses started to appear. One virus was Flashback. It infected hundreds of thousands of Apple computers in 2012.

250,000
Number of Apple computers the Flashback virus infected in 2012.

- Some people believe Apple computers are immune from viruses.
- But viruses can attack any type of computer.
- Hackers tend to attack the most popular computers.

MALWARE

Malware is short for "malicious software." Malware is any kind of program designed to harm a computer. The program usually runs without a user's knowledge. Malware includes viruses, worms, Trojans, rootkits, adware, and spyware.

4

Busted: Ordinary Magnets Erase Hard Drives

In the 1980s, experts warned people not to expose computer hard drives to magnets. Hard drives store information using magnetism. Many thought even the smallest refrigerator magnet could erase all their data. Magnets do affect hard drives. But it takes a very strong magnet to erase one.

Early hard drives were vulnerable to magnets.

A hard drive has two primary parts. The platter is a shiny circular plate of magnetic material. It is divided into billions of tiny areas. The read-write head magnetizes or demagnetizes these areas. It allows information to be stored on the platter. If the area is magnetized, it stores a 1. If it is not, it stores a 0. This is a binary digit, or bit.

Degaussing creates a strong magnetic field that destroys hard drives.

Hard drives contain billions of bits. To demagnetize and erase them all, the magnet needs to be incredibly strong. It can be done, though today's hard drives are designed to resist being erased. But an ordinary kitchen magnet is far too weak. At 50 gauss, it is not strong enough to do any damage. Experts use a tool called a degausser to erase data from disk drives. A typical degausser creates a high-intensity magnetic field. The field destroys all of the areas on the hard drive. After degaussing, the hard drive is unusable.

1,500
Gauss strength needed for a magnet to wipe a hard drive.

- A hard drive stores information using magnetism.
- Ordinary magnets are not strong enough to affect a modern hard drive.
- Experts use degaussers to generate very strong magnetic fields and erase hard drives.

Busted: Batteries Should Be Empty Before Being Recharged

Decades ago, rechargeable batteries needed to be completely empty before they could be recharged. If they were not charged from empty, they lost their capacity to hold a full charge. These batteries were made with nickel. Nickel cadmium (NiCad) batteries were popular in the 1980s.

NiCad batteries had a problem called the memory effect. This type of battery remembered how much it was charged. If a battery was always charged when it was 25 percent full, the battery would remember it needed 75 percent of its capacity. Each time it was charged, the battery lost some of its ability to fully recharge.

In the 1990s, new rechargeable batteries became available. Nickel-metal hydride (NiMH) batteries still had a memory problem. But the

Early rechargeable batteries lost the ability to fully charge over time.

3

Years a lithium-ion battery typically lasts in a cell phone used every day.

- Older rechargeable batteries were made of nickel and needed to be drained before being recharged.
- Newer rechargeable batteries are made of lithium.
- Lithium batteries do not need to be fully discharged before charging.

NEW BATTERY TECHNOLOGY

Solid-state batteries are one of several new battery technologies. Most batteries today, including lithium-ion ones, have liquid cores. The liquid conducts the current from one electrode to the other. Solid state batteries do not have liquid cores. They use layers of metal and other material to conduct the current. These batteries are smaller and less flammable than other types.

issue was not as severe as the issue with NiCad batteries.

Today, most laptops and other devices use lithium-ion or lithium-polymer batteries. Lithium batteries do not suffer from the memory effect. Running the battery down to zero repeatedly can damage lithium batteries. Keeping the battery charged actually makes it last longer.

You should not completely drain a lithium-ion battery before recharging it.

Busted: Cell Phones Can Be Tracked When They Are Turned Off

In 2013, the *Washington Post* reported cell phones could be tracked even when turned off. Most security experts said this was not true. If a modern cell phone is off, it is not broadcasting any identifying information.

Law enforcement can track cell phones two ways. They track cell phones through cell phone tower data. Cell phone towers send out pings to nearby active phones. The phones send signals back to the towers. As a phone moves out of a tower's area, the signal weakens. Another tower picks up the signal. Police can trace a phone's location by combining the data from three different cell towers. But the accuracy of the location varies. Obstacles such as trees and buildings can interrupt the signals.

Today, most cell phones also receive Global Positioning System (GPS)

Law enforcement can find a cell phone by tracking its signal.

signals. Satellites send these signals. More than two dozen GPS satellites currently orbit Earth. Using three of those satellites, a GPS receiver can find a cell phone's location. This is how GPS navigation and tracking works.

To track a phone, cell towers and GPS require the phone to be turned on. However, someone could install malware or a device on a cell phone. The software could trick the user into thinking the device is turned off. Then, police or a hacker could track the phone using cell towers or GPS.

STINGRAY

Law enforcement can also track cell phones with a new device called a Stingray. It mimics a cell phone tower. The device sends out a signal stronger than the nearest tower. This forces all cell phones in the area to connect with the Stingray.

Turning off a cell phone turns off its GPS signal.

11,000
Miles (17,700 km) above Earth that GPS satellites orbit.

- Law enforcement uses cell phone towers and GPS to track cell phone signals.
- Modern cell phones must be powered on to emit these signals.
- Hackers can also install malware to keep phones turned on and reveal their locations.

15

Busted: Private Browsing Is Private

Most Web browsers have a private browsing mode. It erases the digital tracks a user leaves behind. When users exit private mode, it deletes their browsing history. Search history and cookies are erased. Private mode is useful on shared or public computers. Users of the computer will not be able to see the websites others have visited.

However, private browsing does not hide what users do online. Internet service providers and any websites you visit see a computer's unique Internet address. They can see it even when the browser is in private mode.

Private browsing also does not block harmful software. A keylogger is a software program. It records the keys a user types. It saves the information to a protected file.

Web browsers use cookies to track your activity online.

You may browse the Internet in private, but the sites you visit are still tracked.

Hackers use a keylogger to capture passwords. They can also collect other personal information about users.

10

Average minutes a private browsing session lasts.

- Most browsers have a private browsing mode.
- This mode erases the computer's Web and search history as well as cookies and passwords.
- However, the mode does not hide the computer's unique address from the outside world.

ANONYMOUS BROWSING

It is possible to browse the Internet anonymously. To do this, users must hide their computer's unique address. Some services and apps reroute the computer's address through a third party. A Virtual Private Network (VPN) also allows users to browse anonymously.

Busted: Cell Phones Cause Gas Pump Explosions

Many gas stations have signs showing a cell phone with a slash through it. Some local fire codes forbid using electronic devices while pumping gas. Why? Numerous stories on the Internet and elsewhere say gas and electronics do not mix. A spark from a cell phone could ignite gas fumes. This could cause a fire or explosion.

But this fear is based on a myth. Many studies have concluded cell phones do not cause gas pump fires. The Petroleum Equipment Institute has not found any real cases where this happened. The Institute even tried to ignite gas fumes using cell phones. The experiment failed. The Federal Communication Commission agrees with the Institute. It states there is no documented evidence of pump fires caused by cell phones.

A spark can cause gasoline fumes to ignite. Sparks usually come from

Some people believe the gas station is no place for cell phones.

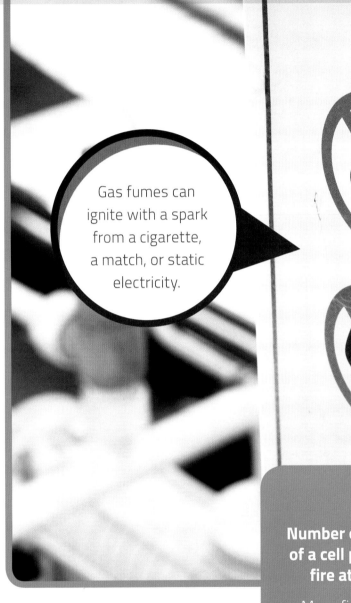

Gas fumes can ignite with a spark from a cigarette, a match, or static electricity.

static electricity. When people get out of their cars, they might build up static electricity. When they touch the gas pump nozzle, a spark from their fingertip might ignite gas fumes.

0
Number of verified cases of a cell phone igniting a fire at a gas pump.

- Many fire codes prohibit using cell phones while pumping gas.
- Several studies prove cell phones cannot ignite gas fumes.
- The real culprit in gas pump fires is static electricity.

Busted: Your Online Activity Can Be Tracked Instantly

TV shows and movies show law enforcement tracking suspects' online activity. The police intercept a suspect's e-mail or chat room message. They read it on their own computer screen. But is this instant tracking really possible?

Not exactly. An Internet service provider (ISP) does log metadata.

It keeps track of a computer's unique address. An ISP can track which computers communicated with other specific computers. Most ISPs collect this data automatically. But they keep it for only a certain amount of time. Typically, no one ever looks at these logs.

Police cannot track websites suspects visit in real time.

6
Minimum number of months ISPs in the United States keep records.

- ISPs collect metadata on all customers.
- Law enforcement agencies can require ISPs to share these records.
- Law enforcement can reconstruct the websites someone visited and make educated guesses about other content, such as e-mails.

However, law enforcement can require ISPs to share these records. In the United States, ISPs can share this data only with the government. With this data, law enforcement can see the websites a user visited. They can also infer whether an e-mail was sent. They can even guess if a suspect watched a movie online. With a lot of work, they can find out who received the message. Law enforcement can find out what someone was looking at online. But it does not happen instantly, as it does on TV.

Once they have records from a suspect's ISP, police can investigate a suspect's online activity.

Busted: Password-Protected Wi-Fi Is Safe

Libraries, coffee shops, and other public places offer free Wi-Fi. Sometimes, free Wi-Fi is protected by a password. Some people might think their private information is safe.

But a Wi-Fi password gives the user access only to the network. Your information may be safe from users *outside* the network. But it is not safe from other users *inside* the network. These users can potentially see your Internet activity. This can include any passwords or credit card

Studying at the coffee shop may be fun, but the Wi-Fi may not be secure.

THINK ABOUT IT

Have you used free public Wi-Fi? What might you do differently in the future to protect yourself while using a public network?

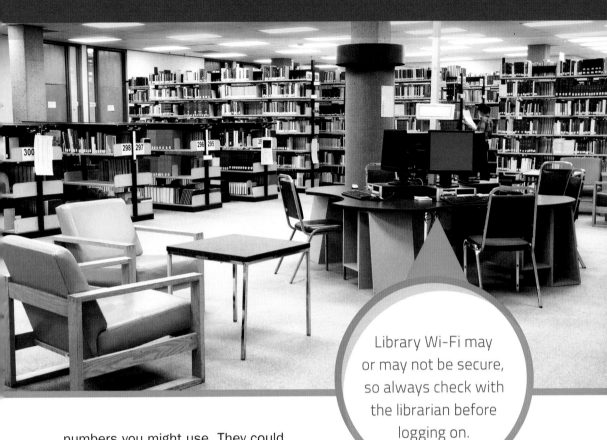

Library Wi-Fi may or may not be secure, so always check with the librarian before logging on.

numbers you might use. They could steal this information or use it in harmful ways.

Hackers can get access to data in two ways. One, they can spoof the Wi-Fi connection. They can set up a fake connection with the same name as the public Wi-Fi. Users do not know they are logging into a counterfeit Wi-Fi network. Hackers can easily monitor the Internet activity on the fake network. They may grab user data with sniffers. A sniffer is an app. It lets a hacker capture all of the Internet traffic on an unsecured network.

39

Percent of US schools with Wi-Fi access in September 2014.

- Many public places offer free Wi-Fi.
- Users are not protected from others on the same Wi-Fi network.
- Hackers can potentially see users' Internet activity on the public Wi-Fi network.

Busted: Hybrid Cars Are Greener to Manufacture than Regular Cars

Hybrid cars have both gasoline and electric motors. Hybrids burn less gas and emit less pollution than purely gas-powered cars do. But critics say these facts do not tell the whole story. They say making a hybrid car creates more pollution. The process uses more energy, too.

In the long run, critics say hybrids are worse for the environment. A 2007 automobile industry report claimed a Hummer was greener than Toyota's hybrid, the Prius.

The critics are partially right. According to the US Department of Energy, manufacturing

In 2007, some people in the auto industry claimed a Hummer was greener than a Prius.

117.5

Number of pounds (53.3 kg) the batteries in a Toyota Prius weigh.

- Hybrid cars use both a gas and electric motor.
- A hybrid car takes more energy to manufacture because of the batteries.
- But the hybrid uses far less energy on the road.

hybrids does use more energy. Most parts of a hybrid are the same as a regular car's parts. The big difference is the batteries. Hybrids need a heavy rack of batteries. The batteries store energy and power the electric motor. They are made of nickel, copper, lithium, and other minerals. These minerals must be mined and transported. Mining and transporting burn fossil fuels and emit greenhouse gases. When a hybrid and a conventional car roll out of the factory, the hybrid has used more energy.

But the hybrid car makes up the difference on the road. The Department of Energy compared conventional and hybrid cars in the course of their lifetimes. Hybrid cars used far less energy than conventional ones used. Hybrids also created far fewer emissions. In the long run, they were better for the environment, not worse.

Over its lifetime, this Prius will be better for the environment than a conventional car.

Busted: Google Can Find Everything on the Web

Google has indexed more Web pages than any other search engine has. It sends out its webcrawlers to find information. The links they find are stored in Google's database. However, they have discovered only a small percentage of the Web. And the Web is only a small portion of the vast Internet.

Google's search engines cannot find all types of files. For instance, Google can find video and images, but only if they are tagged. Google cannot necessarily crawl public or private databases or copyrighted material, such as books. Streaming video dominates more and more of the Internet. Google does not index this type of video.

Google has the largest index of Web pages on the Internet.

Streaming videos, such as those on Netflix, are not indexed by Google.

Google does have the largest index of any of the search engines. But even its webcrawlers and bots have reached only a small percentage of the Web. Google can find Web pages only if they are linked to other ones. Google cannot crawl all rich media types.

0.004
Estimated percentage of the Internet that Google has indexed.

- Google has crawled and indexed more pages than other search engines have.
- Yet Google's spiders have not reached all of the Web.
- And Google cannot find all types of files.

WEBCRAWLERS, SPIDERS, AND BOTS

A webcrawler is a program that sifts through websites. It is also called a spider or bot. The spider builds lists of keywords found on each page. The lists and locations are sent back to the search engine's database. Spiders can crawl up to 100 Web pages per second.

Fact Sheet

- An internet protocol (IP) number is a computer's unique number on the Internet. IP numbers can be static or dynamic. A static IP number is the same every time the computer goes online. A dynamic IP changes every time you log onto the Internet. Most ISPs assign dynamic IP addresses to their customers.

- You can learn what your computer's IP number is. Type "Find IP number" or "What is my IP" in the Google search box. It will provide the IP address in its search results. Like other Web pages, Google tracks your computer's IP address. That is how it can share it with you.

- Hackers, schools, employers, and parents can use keyloggers to see your activity on your computer. Keyloggers capture keystrokes, or what is being typed, on your computer. Most keyloggers are software. But some keyloggers are hardware that can be attached to your keyboard.

- Your wireless network at home is probably safer than the Wi-Fi connection at a local coffee shop. But hackers can still take advantage of your network if it is old or not set up correctly. They can log into your Wi-Fi and launch an attack on another system. The attack will look like it is coming from your IP address.

- Today, most Wi-Fi routers use a strong encryption called Wi-Fi Protected Access 2 (WPA2). Older routers use only WPA or the even older Wired Equivalent Privacy (WEP). Hackers can easily crack these encryptions. Many routers come with default usernames and passwords. Many people fail to change these, which lets hackers easily gain access to your wireless network.

Glossary

bandwidth
Capacity of a network to transfer data.

cookies
Small computer files that store Internet browsing data.

gauss
A unit of measurement that measures magnetism.

hacker
A computer expert who illegally gains access to a computer or network.

metadata
Data stored numerically on a computer.

network
Two or more computers connected to each other.

patented
Obtained the right to make, use, or sell an invention.

rootkit
Malware that gives the user administrative access to a computer.

spyware
Malware that spies on a computer.

Trojan
Malware that disguises itself as a regular program such as a game or app.

For More Information

Books

Hunter, Nick. *How Electric and Hybrid Cars Work*. New York: Gareth Stevens Publishing, 2014.

Smibert, Angie. *12 Great Moments that Changed Internet History*. Mankato, MN: 12-Story Library, 2015.

Turner, Tracey, Andrea Mills, and Clive Gifford. *100 Inventions that Made History: Brilliant Breakthroughs that Shaped Our World*. New York: DK Publishing, 2014.

Visit 12StoryLibrary.com

Scan the code or use your school's login at **12StoryLibrary.com** for recent updates about this topic and a full digital version of this book. Enjoy free access to:

- Digital ebook
- Breaking news updates
- Live content feeds
- Videos, interactive maps, and graphics
- Additional web resources

Note to educators: Visit 12StoryLibrary.com/register to sign up for free premium website access. Enjoy live content plus a full digital version of every 12-Story Library book you own for every student at your school.

Index

About the Author

Angie Smibert is the author of several young adult science fiction novels. She was also a writer and online training developer at NASA's Kennedy Space Center for many, many years. She received NASA's prestigious Silver Snoopy as well as several other awards for her work.

32